AnimalWays

Monkeys

AnimalWays

Monkeys

Marc Zabludoff

Marshall Cavendish
Benchmark
New York

With thanks to Dr. Dan Wharton, director of the Central Park Wildlife Center, for his expert review of this manuscript.

Marshall Cavendish Benchmark
99 White Plains Road
Tarrytown, NY 10591
www.marshallcavendish.us

All Internet sites were available and accurate when sent to press.

Library of Congress Cataloging-in-Publication Data

Zabludoff, Marc.
Monkeys / by Marc Zabludoff.
p. cm. — (Animalways)
Summary: "An exploration of the life cycle, diet, behavior, anatomy, and conservation status of monkeys"—Provided by publisher.
Includes bibliographical references and index.
ISBN 978-0-7614-2535-9
Monkeys—Juvenile literature. I. Title
QL737.P9Z33 2007
599.8—dc22
2007013172

Publisher: Michelle Bisson
Art Director: Anahid Hamparian
Series Designer: Alex Ferrari

Photo research by Candlepants Incorporated

Cover Photo: DILLLC/Corbis

The photographs in this book are used by permission and through the courtesy of:
Peter Arnold Inc.: C. Huetter, 2, 12, 40, back cover; J. Giustina, 9; Ruoso Cyril, 17; Steve Kaufman, 26; P.Oxford, 28; BIOS Denis-Huot M & C, 32; Luiz C. Marigo, 39, 65; Martin Harvey, 48; S. Muller, 50; Fritz Polking, 52; Roland Seitre, 68, 74; Gunter Ziesler, 72; M & C Denis-Huot, 78; A.Shah, 82; Doug Cheeseman, 87. *Corbis*: Martin Harvey, 10, 57; Bojan Brecelj, 15; Steve Kaufman, 18; Thom Lang, 21; Jonathon Blair, 24; James Marshall, 30; Frans Lanting, 35; Gallo Images, 45, 86; Winfried Wisniewski, 60; Staffan Widstrand, 70; David A. Northcott, 77; Tim Chong/Reuters, 81; David G. Wells, 90; Richard T. Nowitz, 92; Bettmann, 95. *The Bridgeman Art Library*: Dinodia, Bombay, India, 16. *Minden Pictures*: SA Team/Foto Natura, 67. *Getty Images*: Robert Ross, 85.

Printed in Malaysia
3 5 6 4 2

Contents

Animal Kingdom

CNIDARIANS

coral

ARTHROPODS
(animals with jointed limbs and external skeleton)

MOLLUSKS

squid

CRUSTACEANS

crab

ARACHNIDS

spider

INSECTS

beetle

MYRIAPODS

centipede

CARNIVORES

lion

SEA MAMMALS

whale

PRIMATES

MONKEY

HERBIVORES
(5 orders)

elephant

ANNELIDS

earthworm

CHORDATES
(animals with
a dorsal
nerve chord)

ECHINODERMS

starfish

VERTEBRATES
(animals with a
backbone)

FISH

BIRDS

MAMMALS

AMPHIBIANS

REPTILES

fish

owl

frog

snake

RODENTS

INSECTIVORES

MARSUPIALS

SMALL MAMMALS
(several orders)

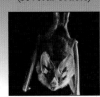

squirrel

mole

koala

bat

1

At Ease in the Trees

High, very high in the trees of this patch of West Africa, the monkeys sit peacefully. For now, there is not even a hint of tension in the air as a group of forty or so animals shifts around in a gentle kaleidoscope of patterns. Against the dark green of the older leaves and the bright green of the younger, splashes of red, gray, and white fur pop out sharply.

There are two different kinds of monkey here, but they are all mixed together. They do not seem to be friends exactly—more like business partners who have known each other for a long time. They are not vying with each other for food or position. They seem simply to have camped out together, comfortably.

The larger ones are Diana monkeys, and they are gorgeous. They are mostly a grayish blue, but they have a luxurious white shawl draping their shoulders and arms. Several are scrambling along the branches, grabbing at ripe fruit as they go, taking quick bites, and chattering happily, almost like birds. One has a

THE EVER-VIGILANT DIANA MONKEYS OF AFRICA ARE OFTEN THE FIRST TO SPOT APPROACHING DANGER, SO OTHER MONKEYS FREQUENTLY SEEK OUT THEIR COMPANY AND FEED NEARBY.

baby clinging tightly to her fur. Nearby, another of these monkeys lies quietly as her fur is thoroughly combed through by her seated companion.

The companion, though, looks different. She is a red colobus monkey, a member of the second group. Her fur is a rich chestnut brown, painted with broad strokes of black down her back and across her legs. Other red colobus monkeys move

RED COLOBUS MONKEYS ARE SLOW-MOVING, BIG-BELLIED LEAF EATERS THAT MUST SPEND MUCH OF THEIR TIME RESTING WHILE THEY DIGEST THEIR FOOD.

slowly through the treetops, munching quietly on tender leaves, while she continues grooming her contented neighbor.

Every so often the red colobus monkeys look up to the very top of the trees, where one of the white-caped Diana males has assumed the pose of a sentry. He scans the forest all around for any signs of danger. But there is nothing worrisome, no reason to sound an alarm—no sign of screeching, diving eagles; no hint of mad chimpanzees on the march. For now, on this warm, peaceful morning, in this one spot in Africa, life is about as perfect as it can get for a bunch of monkeys just trying to get along.

Long-Term Residents

Monkeys have been scampering about the African forest for quite a long time now, longer than most people probably suspect. Monkeys' small ancestors were hanging out in the treetops while huge dinosaurs were still thundering over the Earth. Those ancient relatives were insect eaters and absolutely tiny compared with the meat- or plant-eating giants on the ground below. But they were tougher than one might think. They survived whatever catastrophe wiped out the dinosaurs and went on to establish one of the great branches of the animal kingdom—the branch that eventually sprouted us.

Also contrary to most people's expectations, not all monkeys cavort among the tall trees of South American rain forests or the "jungles" of Africa. Many monkeys actually spend nearly all their time on the ground. Some are a long way from delicate —they are large, intimidating beasts of 100 pounds (45 kg) or more. Some monkeys live not in humid forests but along the edge of arid deserts, atop snow-covered mountains, or in cities and towns. Monkeys occupy not just a narrow slice of tree-dense forests but a broad band of our planet that covers Central

and South America, Africa, India, and southern Asia, from Afghanistan to Japan.

One thing that nearly everyone knows, though, is that with their disturbing resemblance to humans, monkeys are fascinating. Who has looked into the face of a monkey and not been startled by its obvious intelligence? Who has not seen in a monkey's face a reminder of a friend or relative?

We are as easily captivated by monkey behavior as monkey appearance. The ways monkeys seem to interact with one another—as friends, enemies, rivals, partners, bullies, demanding children, and indulgent parents—are so often humanlike that we are tempted to view a monkey's mind and thoughts as simpler versions of our own. On the other hand, throughout history, many people have been tempted to see monkeys as something more than human.

Monkeys Among the Pharaohs

The earliest records we have of human attitudes toward monkeys come from the ancient Egyptians. The monkey they knew best was the hamadryas baboon, and its image appeared in Egyptian carvings and hieroglyphs as far back as 5,000 years ago. The baboon was a sacred animal to the Egyptians. It was often portrayed as the companion and servant of Thoth, the god of writing and measurement. In this divine role, the baboon was often shown seated on a throne, watching over the work of royal scribes as they recorded the wishes of princes and kings. Baboons are also shown guarding the gates to the underworld, weighing the hearts of the dead to determine if they are worthy of passing through to the afterlife.

Ancient Egypt flourished for thousands of years, and the exact role that baboons played in Egyptian religion changed with the centuries. Sometimes Thoth himself was portrayed as having the head of a baboon. Often a baboon head topped the figure of a lesser god named Hapi. Frequently baboons were shown worshipping the moon or the sun. But no matter what its precise identity or duties were thought to be, the ancient Egyptians saw in this large monkey a reflection of the gods' power. To show their respect, when a sacred baboon died, the Egyptians mummified it and buried it in a tomb.

Monkey Tales of Asia

Many ancient peoples of Asia, noting the strikingly human features of monkeys' hands, faces, and expressions, assumed that monkeys, like people, were of primary importance to the gods. In the stories the people created, monkeys sometimes earn the respect or gratitude of the gods and receive great powers as a reward. In some Asian cultures, as in Egypt, monkeys were seen as companions and helpers to the gods, and nearly as gods themselves.

In the myths of India, Hanuman was the monkey god who helped rescue Sita, the wife of the god Rama; she had been kidnapped by Rama's rivals and taken to Sri Lanka. One version of the myth relates that while on his mission, Hanuman was forced to set fire to the town in which Sita was held captive. He and Sita escaped, but the fire scorched his hands, feet, and face. Another version claims that in Sri Lanka, Hanuman discovered the sacred mango, a fruit previously unknown. Delighted with the sweet fruit—as any monkey would be—Hanuman stole it and brought it back to India. When the theft was discovered, Hanuman was sentenced to be burned. The fire was lit, but Hanuman beat at the flames until he managed to extinguish them. However, as in the first story, his hands, feet, and face were blackened. Today, according to tradition, all Hanuman langurs—a type of monkey found throughout India and named for the burned god—still carry the telltale black marks of their ancestor's ordeal.

Monkey gods and princes figure in many Asian tales. One of the best known is the Chinese tale of the monkey king. Although the story is probably much older, it was first recorded in a novel called *Journey to the West*, written in the 1500s. It is an elaborately complicated tale, filled with the adventures of a badly behaved monkey ruler. Throughout the long story of the monkey's battle with the gods, the monkey king is pictured as a rebellious creature. He is clever but, in the beginning, he is not very wise, and he uses his intelligence mainly to cause trouble.

Eventually the monkey king is enlisted to help protect a holy man traveling to India. Fighting all the way, fending off armies of demons, the monkey king succeeds in his task, and the man

TO THE ANCIENT EGYPTIANS, THE BABOON WAS CLOSELY CONNECTED TO THE GODS. THIS ANIMAL, WITH ITS ARMS RAISED AND PALMS TURNED OUTWARD, WAS PAINTED IN A TYPICAL POSE OF WORSHIP.

brings back the holy books of Buddhism to China. By the end of the journey, the monkey king has gained great powers. He has learned how to change himself into seventy-two different forms, from a tree to a lion to an insect. He can jump thousands of miles in a single leap. More important, he has also gained wisdom. His argumentative nature has been tamed, and he has become humble.

HANUMAN, THE MONKEY GOD, IS A REVERED FIGURE IN HINDU MYTHS AND PLAYS A CENTRAL ROLE IN MANY ADVENTURE TALES.

HANUMAN LANGURS ARE FOUND THROUGHOUT INDIA. THEIR TRADITIONAL ASSOCIA-
TION WITH THE MONKEY GOD GIVES THEM SPECIAL STATUS, AND THEY ARE NEARLY
ALWAYS PROTECTED AND FED.

Versions of the monkey king pop up as heroes in many different tales, usually as warriors who come to help someone out in an overwhelming battle. Likewise, the association of monkeys with Buddhist tradition appears in many Asian artworks. In Japan, a wood carving on a seventeenth-century Buddhist temple depicts three monkeys, one with its hands covering its ears, another covering its mouth, the third covering its eyes. The image of the "three wise monkeys" has become familiar around the world as the portrayal of the teaching to "hear, speak, and see no evil."

THIS CARVING OF THE THREE WISE MONKEYS, IN NIKKO, JAPAN, DATES BACK TO THE 1600s. BUT THE IMAGE MAY HAVE ORIGINATED AT LEAST EIGHT CENTURIES EARLIER, IN CHINA.

Mayan Monkeys

Everywhere monkeys lived, people lived too, and they crafted myths about these mysterious tree-dwelling creatures. To the Maya, building their civilization amid the forests of southern Mexico and Central America, monkeys were the representatives of the gods in many aspects of life and death. Among the Mayan gods were two brothers known simply as Howler Monkey and Spider Monkey. Together they ruled over such purely human activities as music, dance, sculpture, and (as in Egypt) writing. Some stories link Spider Monkey to the spirit of trickery and fun, while Howler Monkey represents the idea of work and duty. Both characteristics were seen as being part of human nature.

Another Mayan tradition holds that when the gods created the world, monkeys were one of their early experiments at creating humans. The results were close to what the gods desired but not perfect, so people eventually joined the monkeys on Earth.

Monkeys Around the World

Monkeys appeared as characters in many folktales originating in Africa, and they traveled west along with the Africans who were tragically brought to the Americas as slaves. So the monkey tales were told in the islands of the Caribbean and the American South, places where no monkeys lived, and it is partly from them that we get our notions of what a monkey is. In many of the stories, monkeys are mischievous tricksters or disrespectful creatures who are constantly getting into trouble—often as the result of their curious, unrestrained nature.

In tale after tale, no matter what part of the world it comes from, the monkey appears as a human in a strange form, with a human's thoughts, emotions, and desires. In some ways the myths and stories are true: monkeys indeed are smart and curious. Some are in fact very rebellious, some are mischievous, and some are fierce warriors. The reality, however, is that monkeys are not scaled-down people. Although they are big-brained, their minds are very different from our own, and we cannot understand them in human terms. But we do not need to see monkeys as humanlike in order to find them interesting. Just understanding them in their own terms is challenging enough.

2 A Brief History of Monkeys

What kind of animals are monkeys exactly? Where precisely do they fit on the great tree of life, and why do they have such a disturbing similarity to us?

To answer these questions, we must first have a basic understanding of how scientists organize the messy multitude of life forms found in the world. They start by sorting everything into five broad categories, called kingdoms, one of which is the kingdom that contains all animals. (The other four kingdoms hold the plants, fungi, bacteria, and the mostly single-celled organisms called protoctists.) Each kingdom then contains within it a series of smaller and smaller categories called, in order: phylum, class, order, family, genus, and species.

NEW WORLD MONKEYS, LIKE THIS WHITE-FACED CAPUCHIN FROM COSTA RICA, ARE ALL TREE DWELLERS AND THEY RARELY SPEND ANY TIME ON THE GROUND.

Order in the Monkey House

This may sound confusing, but in the case of monkeys it will seem familiar very quickly. Monkeys, first of all, are mammals, members of the class Mammalia, as we humans are. All mammals share certain characteristics that tie them together as a group. For example, they all have hair or fur (as opposed to scales or feathers), the females give birth to live young (rather than lay eggs), and they feed their young with milk.

The class of mammals is further divided into a number of different orders. One order, for example, contains all the sharp-toothed carnivores, or meat eaters, such as lions and wolves, along with their slightly less ferocious relatives, housecats and dogs. Another order contains all the hoofed mammals, from hippos to horses. Monkeys belong to the order called Primates. Along with the monkeys in the Primate order are the prosimians—a large group of small-bodied, big-eyed tree dwellers—and the apes. The apes include the long-armed, tree-swinging gibbons, which are also known as the lesser apes, and the orangutans, gorillas, chimpanzees, and humans, which make up the great apes. Some people find it disturbing to be lumped together with a bunch of apes, so other descriptions of the primates show the order to be made of four groups—prosimians, monkeys, apes, and humans—instead of three.

Another way of organizing the primates is to divide them into two groups. One group includes only the prosimians, animals such as lemurs and lorises. The other group is called the anthropoids, which means "humanlike," and it includes the monkeys, apes, and us. The anthropoids are again divided into two groups: the first is made up of only the New World monkeys, meaning those that come from Central and South America. (The New World was the name the early European explorers gave to the Americas). The other group is the Old

World anthropoids, and it includes all the monkeys of Africa and Asia, all the apes, and once again, us.

No matter how you arrange the primates, however, the outcome is always the same—on the tree of life, monkeys and people are near neighbors, sitting together on a single limb. What that means is that we share a common history, a large number of common ancestors, and many physical features. In fact what it really means is that we and the monkeys are not just neighbors but cousins. Not the closest of cousins—we are much more closely related to chimpanzees and the other apes than to monkeys. But still, we are close enough to see a sometimes disturbing likeness.

Primate Evolution

The history of the primates goes back some 70 million years, to a time when beasts like *Tyrannosaurus rex* were still roaming the Earth. Probably unnoticed by any of the dinosaurs, small squirrel-sized primate ancestors were crawling along branches grabbing as many insects as they could catch while living a life in the trees. These animals, known as plesiadapids, were nocturnal (active mainly at night), a lifestyle that helped them avoid daytime predators. They had small brains, sharp biting teeth like those of a rat, and may have glided between trees using flaps of skin stretched between their arms and legs.

The plesiadapids thrived for about 15 million years, and developed into more than 100 species, or distinct types. Some were tiny, weighing only a third of an ounce (10 g). Others grew to a hefty 6.5 pounds (3 kg). But around 55 million years ago, 10 million years after the dinosaurs went extinct, the plesiadapids followed suit. Earth at that time was going through a major climate change. Around the world, temperatures were rising, and they soon hovered around 95 degrees F (35 degrees C). This

A 49 MILLION-YEAR-OLD FOSSIL FROM GERMANY SHOWS THE TELLTALE HAND BONES OF A PRIMATE ANCESTOR THAT LIVED IN WHAT WAS THEN A HOT, FORESTED ENVIRONMENT.

was a world too hot for the plesiadapids but apparently just right for their descendants, known to paleontologists as the adapids.

The adapids were the first true primates. They were cat-sized creatures, with many of the features that characterize primates today. For example, they had flat nails on their toes instead of pointed claws. More important, they had opposable big toes, which means that the tip of the big toe could curl around toward the tips of the other toes. This allowed them to grip the branches they walked on tightly. Most important, the adapids had big brains and eyes on the front of their heads rather than on the sides.

In the hothouse climate, the adapids did well. By 40 million years ago, more than 180 species had developed. Some ate fruit as well as insects, and some were active during the day instead of at night.

Then the planet began to cool again. Temperatures plunged until, about 30 million years ago, the average global temperature was down to just 41 degrees F (5 degrees C). As the northern and southern parts of the planet grew colder, the tropical forests shrank back toward the warmer equator. The range of the primates shrank with the forests in which they lived.

Paleontologists do not know exactly when the first animal that looked like a monkey or an ape appeared. They have not yet found the fossils marking the event. But they have found fossils from 35 million years ago that prove that monkey ancestors were then living along the edge of what is now the Egyptian desert, but what was then a lush, tropical forest.

These animals were different from the adapids that came before them. They were primarily fruit eaters and completely day-active animals. Nocturnal animals must rely on their hearing and sense of smell to find their way in the world. These new animals relied chiefly on their vision. They were the first anthropoids, the direct ancestors of monkeys and apes.

The monkeys themselves show up sometime around 25 million years ago. At first they were a minor branch of the family. Apes were far more common. But around 15 million years ago, after a long period of gradual warming, Earth began changing again, becoming drier and cooler.

An African patas monkey is a tough animal, able to survive along the edges of some of the harshest, driest deserts on Earth.

Once again the forest home of the primates changed. The forests became less dense, with more space between trees. A new, more open woodland environment appeared, especially in Africa, where the early monkeys lived. Fewer trees in a smaller forest, of course, meant a smaller supply of fruit. But this affected the apes much more than the monkeys.

Not only did the smaller monkeys need less food than the apes, but the monkeys had also developed the ability to digest fruit that was not quite ripe. Apes (and people) cannot eat unripe fruit without getting a stomachache. Because the monkeys could, they were able to dine on the available food first. So, while ape numbers dwindled, monkey numbers soared. With the one notable exception of humans, that inequality exists to this day.

Over the past 25 million years, monkeys have developed into some 200 species in both the Old World and the New. Interestingly, Old World monkeys are more closely related to apes than they are to their American cousins. The New World monkeys evolved from some primate ancestor that traveled to South America sometime after the Egyptian anthropoids appeared but before the first African monkeys evolved. It is confusing, to be sure, but it is the only way to explain the differences between the two monkey groups.

Old World vs. New

Although American monkeys and African and Asian monkeys are clearly the same kind of animal, they display several physical differences. Among them are these:

New World monkeys generally have wide nostrils that face sideways. Old World monkeys have narrow noses and nostrils that point downward.

New World monkeys have 36 teeth. Old World monkeys have 32.

All New World monkeys are dedicated tree dwellers. Many Old World monkeys live mostly on the ground.

A number of New World monkeys have prehensile tails—that is, tails that can curl around and grab something tightly. No Old World monkey has such a tail.

Except for that last item, all that was said about Old World monkeys could also be said about apes. But the tail is a telltale, if trivial, distinction between monkeys and apes. Monkeys have tails, apes do not. Apes are also smarter than monkeys, as a rule. But that difference is not always so apparent.

DESPITE ITS DELICATE APPEARANCE, THE GOLDEN SNUB-NOSED MONKEY CAN EASILY HANDLE THE SNOW AND COLD OF WESTERN CHINA'S TALL MOUNTAINS.

Monkey Habitats

With the exception of humans, monkeys have spread farther than any other primate. Notably, they are the only nonhuman primate to have made a home in the Americas. But for the most part monkeys have remained faithful to their primate heritage, and the overwhelming majority of them are creatures of the tropics. Huge areas of the world remain monkey-free, including Australia, New Zealand, North America, northern Asia, and all of Europe, except for the island of Gibraltar, at Europe's southernmost tip, where a colony of monkeys has lived since at least the days of the ancient Romans.

In areas where the monkeys do live, the greatest number of species are found in the tropical rain forests. The farther one travels from the equator, the fewer monkey species one will find. This pattern makes sense in light of the monkeys' heavy dependence on a diet of fruit and leaves. In cooler temperate forests, these foods may be available only during spring and summer.

Still, some monkeys have managed to forge a life for themselves in habitats that do not at first appear to be at all well suited for them. In Africa, baboons have become highly successful residents of the savanna—areas of wide grassy plains broken up by occasional clumps of acacia trees. They are joined in this sometimes sun-baked landscape by ground-dwelling patas monkeys. Patas monkeys can survive in near-deserts, and they live right along the edge of the Sahara. Hamadryas baboons, meanwhile, live in the dry, rocky regions of southern Arabia.

Vervet monkeys too live on the savanna and they have spread across much of sub-Saharan Africa. However, these monkeys are not as adapted to life on the ground as the baboons are, and they spend part of their time in trees. They prefer to stay close to strips of forest that run along rivers and streams.

Some monkeys have found a way to live in much cooler climates. The Japanese macaques are the northernmost monkeys, bedding down in the snowy mountains of northern Japan. Hanuman langurs can handle the snow, too, high in the Himalayas. Harsh mountains also provide a home for the snub-nosed monkeys of western China and the Barbary macaques of Morocco.

BECAUSE MONKEYS CAN SO EASILY TELL JUST WHEN A FRUIT IS RIPE, A FEW—SUCH AS THIS MACAQUE—HAVE BEEN TRAINED TO WORK AS COCONUT PICKERS.

Finding Food

Most monkeys will eat a lot of different foods, though they all have their preferences. However, there are four main types of food that give monkeys everything they need: fruits and seeds; insects and small animals; leaves and flowers; and sap and gum, from trees. There is also grass, but this forms the chief food only of the gelada baboons in the mountains of Ethiopia.

Fruit tops the list. Monkeys love fruit, but you might not know that from watching them eat. Monkeys are notoriously wasteful fruit pickers. They often grab a fruit from a tree, take one or two quick bites, then toss the rest away after deciding that it is not ripe enough for their taste. Why? A monkey's eating habits grow out of its physical abilities and its need to make the best of whatever is available. Monkeys are actually very good at discerning just when fruits are ripe enough to eat. They can eat them earlier, but they prefer to wait for the sweeter, fully ripened variety. Yet if they wait too long, they may lose the fruit to a competitor. So they play a game of compromise, snatching fruit early and eating only the best part of it rather than risk losing the whole thing.

Fruit, though, cannot form their entire diet because it does not provide them with all the nutrients they need. For a well-balanced diet, monkeys have to turn to other sources. Smaller monkeys turn to insects, which are nearly always around, high in protein, and low in fat. But they are usually small, and a large animal would have to eat a lot of them. So bigger monkeys turn to leaves. Many monkeys eat leaves as their primary food, but nearly all monkeys eat leaves occasionally. They usually stick to the young tender ones, though. Plants protect their leaves, making them hard to digest. The older leaves are often very bitter tasting, filled with chemicals that cause most animals to vomit.

IN ADDITION TO FRUIT, MANY MONKEYS EAT A VARIETY OF INSECTS AND SMALL ANI-MALS. SOME, LIKE THIS BABOON, WILL HUNT PREY AS LARGE AS A YOUNG GAZELLE.

Some monkeys also like to eat tree sap and gum, which is a sweet, sticky substance that oozes out of trees when they are injured. Gum is soft at first, but it quickly turns hard when exposed to air, so monkeys have to get it while it is fresh. New World marmosets especially love gum, and they will bite holes in trees to get some.

Monkeys are often categorized as fruit eaters, seed eaters, or leaf eaters, but most monkeys are opportunists, taking advantage of changing conditions. New World capuchins are a good example. They are usually fruit eaters but they will frequently branch out into other food groups. Often they will go on a frantic hunt for protein. They will rip through the trees searching for tarantulas, giant cockroaches, lizards, or tree frogs. They will even come out of the trees and hunt for mice on the ground. If they find one, they kill it by smashing it against a tree.

In Africa, mangabeys rely heavily on fruits and flowers. But they too will at times start ripping the bark off of trees, looking for any six- or eight-legged thing crawling beneath it. They also hunt for birds' nests, devouring both eggs and nestlings if they find them.

Anyone who thinks of monkeys as peaceful vegetarians should examine the diet of savanna-dwelling baboons. These big monkeys eat nearly everything all the time, and they will eat animals whenever they can. Their prey includes ground-nesting birds, rabbits, baby antelope, and other monkeys, such as young vervets. In Kenya, baboons have been seen hunting gazelles as a group, with some baboons driving a gazelle into the waiting arms of others.

In Asia, long-tailed macaques living in mangrove swamps eat crabs. So do African green monkeys. In South America, those opportunistic capuchins, if they live near the ocean, eat oysters.

3 Monkey Bodies

Physically, all primates are so similar that it is easy to explain how a monkey's body works by saying simply that it is basically just like ours. It is worthwhile, though, to go through the monkey's design part by part to highlight those aspects that are different from our own or those that make all primates such hardy creatures.

Skeleton and Teeth

Monkeys have inherited the bony support structure of their bodies from their primate ancestors, animals that evolved for life in the trees. However, something similar can be said for all mammals, even elephants and whales. The ancestors of primates were not the only small mammals back in the age of the dinosaurs. The key difference between primates and all other mammals is that primates have stuck pretty close to the original mammal design while other mammals have become ever more specialized. Cows and horses lost their individual toes and grew

A WOOLLY SPIDER MONKEY, OR MURIQUI, HAS LONG ARMS AND A GRASPING TAIL THAT ENABLE IT TO SWING EFFORTLESSLY FROM BRANCH TO BRANCH.

A MONKEY'S SKELETON IS VERY MUCH LIKE A HUMAN'S, THOUGH IT IS NOT IDENTICAL. ONE BIG DIFFERENCE IS IN THE SHAPE OF THE SKULL. ANOTHER IS IN THE HIP BONES, WHICH HAD TO CHANGE AS HUMAN ANCESTORS STARTED WALKING ON TWO FEET RATHER THAN FOUR.

hooves. Whales lost their rear limbs entirely and saw their front limbs change into flippers. Antelopes, anteaters, giraffes, walruses, wolves, otters, bears, camels—all grew bodies very different from those of their ancestors. Primates did not.

Monkeys generally still have five separate fingers and toes that work so well for climbing and running in trees. They still have the strong collarbone that lets them hang from a branch without pulling apart their shoulders. They still have the two separate bones in their forearms that let them rotate their hands. Critically, they have their opposable big toes and thumbs that let them grab tree limbs and manipulate objects with ease.

The biggest change in the monkey skeleton is in the skull. Compared with their early ancestors, monkeys have a shorter snout, more forward-pointing eyes, and much more room for a brain—just as we do.

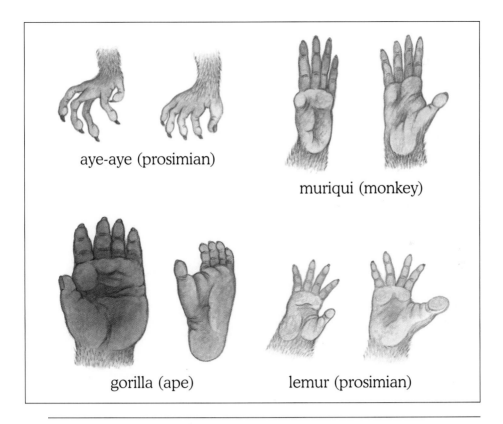

aye-aye (prosimian)

muriqui (monkey)

gorilla (ape)

lemur (prosimian)

PRIMATE FINGERS (LEFT) AND TOES (RIGHT) ARE GENERALLY BUILT FOR CLIMBING AND GRASPING. OPPOSABLE THUMBS ALLOW THEM TO HANDLE OBJECTS MUCH MORE EASILY THAN OTHER MAMMALS.

Because most monkeys are omnivores, which means that they eat almost everything, they have a mouth full of all-purpose teeth. They have biting incisors in front, pointed canines on the sides, and blocky premolars and molars further back. (New World monkeys, though, have four more premolars than Old World monkeys.) Their canine teeth are much larger and sharper than ours are, however.

Tail

All monkeys, with the curious exception of the Barbary macaque, have tails. Species that live on the ground tend to have shorter tails, and species that live in the trees tend to have longer tails. Only certain New World species have fully prehensile tails that can act as a "fifth hand." On these monkeys, a long section of the tail has no fur on the underside. The bare skin allows monkeys to get a better grip on things. All other tree-dwelling monkeys use their tails for balance or as an "air brake" to slow them down when leaping between branches or trees.

Arms and Legs

The length of a monkey's limbs depends on its lifestyle. Monkeys that need to scramble nimbly along branches have relatively short arms and legs, while monkeys that walk and run on the ground have longer ones. In both cases, all the limbs are about the same length. Those proportions change in monkeys that are exceptional jumpers, such as pygmy marmosets—they have longer legs. Likewise, monkeys that are terrific swingers, such as spider monkeys, have arms longer than their legs.

IN THE AMAZON, QUIET UAKARIS MIGHT PASS UNNOTICED WERE IT NOT FOR THEIR BRIGHT FACES. THEIR CRIMSON SKIN IS ACTUALLY A SIGN OF HEALTH. PALE UAKARIS ARE USUALLY ILL.

Skin and Fur

All monkeys are covered with fur, but it comes in a wide range of colors: black, grays, yellows, browns, silver, gold, red, white, and blue. Their furry coat is also decorated with a great variety of patterns. The different looks make it easy for monkeys to recognize members of their own species by sight alone. Many other mammals use smell.

Not all of a monkey's body is covered in fur. Many monkeys have bare skin around the face, and often this skin is colored brightly. The uakari, for example, has a face so red that it appears to be permanently sunburned. Facial skin may also

In many monkey species, males and females differ in size or color. Only mature black howler males, for example, have black fur; females and youngsters are much lighter.

have dramatic patterns. Mandrill males, for example, have spectacular red snouts set off by blue and white racing stripes.

To the endless amusement of zoo-visiting children, quite a few monkeys also have brightly colored sexual organs and rear ends. Mandrills have blue bottoms, for instance, while baboons have red ones. Some Old World monkeys that spend a lot of time sitting also have rears with patches of bare, very tough skin. These are like calluses, and they protect the monkey from injury.

Sexual Dimorphism

Among many animals, males and females are different in size. The phenomenon is called sexual dimorphism, and it is commonly exhibited by monkeys. Males are often larger than females, and they have larger canine teeth. The difference is especially noticeable in baboon males, which may be twice as big as the females. Males may also have different colored fur. Black howler males are indeed black, for example, but female black howlers are actually a light olive gray or brown. Male howlers also have a long cape of fur that drapes over their shoulders. Not all monkeys follow this pattern, however. Among marmosets and tamarins, the smallest of the New World monkeys, males and females are very similar.

Internal Systems

The insides of a monkey are not essentially different from the insides of a human. In some cases, however, the digestive system differs a bit. Monkeys that are primarily leaf eaters, such as South American howlers, have large stomachs filled with bacteria that break down their hard-to-digest food and release its nutrients. Leaf-eating African colobus monkeys and Asian langurs have more complex stomachs that are divided into two parts. The upper part is loaded with the bacteria that break down the leaves' cell walls. The food then passes to the lower part of the stomach, which is kept separated from the upper part. This chamber is filled with digestive fluids that would kill the bacteria. They further break down the food before passing it on to a very long intestine that gives the monkey's body a lot of time to absorb everything it can from its diet of leaves. To make room for all this digestive machinery, these monkeys have a characteristic pot belly.

Senses

As with so much else about monkeys, the range of their senses is extraordinarily familiar to us since we share much of their evolutionary past. For both humans and monkeys, a short snout and small ears reflect a reduced dependence on the senses of smell and hearing. At the same time, the forward-facing eyes signal an increased dependence on vision.

Sensitive hearing and smell are essential for animals navigating a dark, nighttime forest. But as the monkeys' ancestors gave up their nocturnal lifestyle, they did not need especially big ears and noses. In the daylight, good eyesight became much more critical to them.

Unlike many other mammals, monkeys see the world in full color, which is a valuable ability for an animal trying to spot which tree has the ripest fruit before anyone else does. Even more valuable is the ability to see the world in three dimensions. All primates can do this as a result of their eyes position at the front of their head rather than on the sides. To see truly in 3D, an animal must have overlap between what its right eye is seeing and what its left eye is seeing. The more the eyes are placed to the sides, the less overlap there is, and the flatter the world appears. The more the eyes are at the front, pointing forward, the more overlap there is, and the dimension of depth is added to the picture. Seeing the world in 3D means that you have the ability to judge how far away something is—a very useful thing to know if you are leaping between trees, high above the ground.

Monkeys also have an unusually refined sense of touch that allows them to manipulate objects easily. Their hands and feet and, especially, the tips of their fingers are intricately dotted with nerve endings. So is the tip of a New World monkey's prehensile tail.

Making sense of all the information provided by the senses is the monkey's brain. Primates all have complex brains, the most complex of all the animals. Broadly speaking, the brains of monkeys are in the middle of the primate range. They are less complex than those of chimpanzees and other apes, more complex than those of lemurs and other prosimians. Those large, complicated brains play a large role in shaping their interesting lives. They also play a large role in shaping the monkeys' relationship with us, their large primate cousins.

4 Monkey Lives

What really makes the monkeys different is not their bodies. It is their behavior. Two attributes distinguish the monkeys from other mammals: their intelligence and their extremely social nature, and the two are intricately connected.

Monkeys live in a complicated tangle of relationships that are vital to their health and survival. The details vary from one species to the next, but the essential fact remains: few monkeys are mentally built to live alone.

All monkeys live with company and usually a lot of it. The size and organization of a monkey group, or troop, vary. They depend on the monkey's normal habitat and how much food is available, among other factors. But in very general terms, primatologists—scientists who specialize in the study of primates—recognize three kinds of monkey groups.

First, there are family groups, made up of a single adult male, a single adult female, and all their growing youngsters. This kind of organization is found primarily among New World sakis, titis, and owl monkeys. It is far less common among Old World monkeys, but there are a few species that live this way.

GELADAS ARE NEVER ALONE—THEY FEED ON HIGH GRASSLANDS IN FAMILY GROUPS, THEN GATHER BY THE HUNDREDS TO RETURN TO THE STEEP CLIFFS WHERE THEY SLEEP.

Second, there are one-male groups, made up of a single adult male, several females, and their young. As with the family groups, the youngsters continue to live with the adults until they reach maturity. At that point, usually the males leave and form groups of their own. In a few species, such as the muriqui (also called the woolly spider monkey) of South America, the females are the ones that leave. But this is rare. A number of Old World monkeys prefer the one-male model for their groups. Among them are guenons, the grass-eating gelada baboons of Ethiopia, and the pink-faced hamadryas baboons. Just because a troop has only one adult male, incidentally, does not necessarily mean that the male is the leader of the troop in any real way. In some species, dominant females call the shots.

Finally, there are multimale groups, made up of several males, many more females (about two females for each male), and, of course, all their many offspring. This may be the most common form of monkey society. It is certainly the form found most often in the Americas, and it characterizes the social organization of howlers, capuchins, marmosets, spider monkeys, and squirrel monkeys. A great many Old World monkeys also live in multimale groups. Among them are most baboons, langurs, and macaques.

By living in groups, monkeys are better able to watch out for danger and defend themselves against predators. That is the positive side. The negative side is that the more members there are in a group, the more competition there is for food. The result is that for monkeys, as for humans, social life is complicated. Monkeys compete with each other and depend on each other at the same time. Each monkey is working for its own benefit so it has to know which other members of the group may stand in its way. It also has to know which other monkeys it can count on if it needs help.

For most monkeys, life is a group enterprise in which each individual is enmeshed in a net of social rules. The rules determine who gets the best food, who will defend the group against attack, who must stay with the group and who may leave, who may join the group, and most important, who gets to have babies. In some monkey societies, the rules are rather relaxed. This most often seems to be the case in species that are entirely tree dwelling. African mangabeys, for example, generally live in groups headed by one male. But he does not exercise very much control over the activities of the group. Members come and go frequently.

Monkeys that live on the ground, on the other hand, tend to have very tightly controlled societies. Baboons, for instance, usually live in troops led by several males that exert strict control over all the other members. It is not common for any baboons to leave the group or for new members to join.

Why do tree dwellers seem more relaxed and ground dwellers more strict? Most likely, the different group structures are a consequence of the monkeys' different needs for security. Primates evolved as tree dwellers because trees were relatively safe places for them to live. Trees remain safe today. Monkeys in trees do face danger from predators, of course, most notably from large birds of prey, such as eagles. But big birds cannot always maneuver so easily through dense leaves and branches, and most tree dwellers are able to avoid capture. The danger is much greater for monkeys on the open ground, which presents no obstacles to a diving bird. Ground-dwelling baboons and patas monkeys are also much more vulnerable to attack by leopards and other large cats. Because of the need for constant vigilance, ground-dwelling monkeys form groups with tighter structures in which every member knows its place and its duty to the group.

LEOPARDS CAN CLIMB TREES, BUT THEY ARE NOT AS NIMBLE AS TREE-DWELLING MONKEYS. THESE BIG CATS POSE MORE OF A DANGER TO GROUND-DWELLING MONKEYS, SUCH AS BABOONS.

As with humans, though, it is not always easy for monkeys to get along with one another. Among other complicating factors, not all monkeys are born equal in size, strength, or personality. In most monkey societies, certain members of a group will be dominant. They are the leaders, and any monkey that does not pay them proper respect risks physical punishment or less access to food. Often there is not just one dominant member of the group but several, and many others who rank higher or lower on the ladder of command. As a result, monkeys must spend a lot of time making sure they stay on the good side of all the monkeys that outrank them. They also must make sure that the group as a whole does not break apart, so even low-ranking monkeys have to be kept satisfied. All monkeys must find a way to make sure they are safe within the group, and the way they do this is through grooming.

Grooming

Anyone who has ever observed monkeys has seen them busily grooming each other. One monkey sits or lies calmly while a companion carefully combs through its fur with its fingers, picking out any bits of food, dead skin, or insects it finds. This is an important practice for monkeys because it keeps their bodies clean and free of biting insects. It is also pleasurable for them. They enjoy the care and attention and the contact with others. Most important, though, grooming is how monkeys keep allies within the troop. In the monkey world, friendship is literally a case of "you scratch my back, and I'll scratch yours." This is most evident among females living in multimale groups. Generally the females stay with the same troop for their entire lives. They know one another well, and each female is aware of the others' strengths and weaknesses. Like children who have

gone through all the years of elementary and middle school together, they know who they can push around and who they must watch out for. To keep from being ganged up on, every one of these monkeys needs the support of others. They get it by establishing grooming relationships with other females that ensure that they will not be forced to defend themselves alone.

Males also need allies within the troop, and they often establish grooming partnerships with other males. A dominant male baboon, for example, is less vulnerable to attack by an ambitious youngster if he has another large male by his side. Knowing whom to groom is a skill that all monkeys must learn. Such social sophistication will be needed by adolescents if they leave the group and attempt to join a new one. These grooming skills are the monkey equivalent of human manners. Only by displaying the proper willingness to groom others will a monkey be accepted by a new group.

The degree to which monkeys need to form tight bonds with one another depends on many factors. Even within a single species, different groups behave differently. It often all comes down to food. When there is plenty of food around, competition is low and the bonds between monkeys are loose. When food is more scarce, the struggles between individuals heat up, and the need for keeping the group together, through peaceful grooming, increases.

Communication

Social animals need ways to keep in touch, and monkeys use sounds and body movements to communicate with other members of their group. In addition, much more so than other animals, monkeys employ a large number of facial expressions to display their intentions and emotions.

The amount of "chatter" that goes on among monkeys varies with their lifestyles. Monkeys that routinely scamper among the leafy treetops are often hidden from one another and they use their voices to make sure the troop stays together. Many New World monkeys are especially noisy forest residents. Small marmosets call to each other constantly, nearly twittering like birds as they scramble through the branches.

AFRICAN VERVETS ARE AMONG THE MOST VOCAL OF ALL MONKEYS, USING A LARGE
VARIETY OF CALLS TO COMMUNICATE WITH OTHER MEMBERS OF THE TROOP.

Squirrel monkey females are probably the most talkative of
the New World monkeys. They seem to get upset if they are not
in constant contact as they move through the forest, and they

call out with high-pitched "peeps" whenever they loose sight of one another. A peep always brings an immediate response from another troop member. Squirrel monkeys also use other sounds with other meanings. The females that direct the troop begin to "twitter" when they want the others to start moving. A third sound, known as a "chuck," is a call used only between close female friends.

Like many animals, some monkey species call out simply to announce their presence and to warn others to stay away from their territory. South American howlers are especially noted for their skill in this practice.

Monkeys do not really have language. They do not have large vocabularies of different-sounding words that they can combine into sentences of varied meaning. But they sometimes seem to come close. Vervet monkeys in Africa have an especially subtle group of sounds used to warn troop members of danger. Because vervets spend time both in trees and on the ground, they must be alert for different types of enemies: leopards and snakes, for example, on land, eagles and other large birds of prey in the trees. Accordingly, they have different kinds of alarm calls. A vervet spotting a big cat stalking the troop will quickly yell out the "Leopard!" call, sending all the monkeys racing up into the trees and out to the ends of branches too thin to support a large cat. A vervet that spies a large predatory bird will let loose with an "Eagle!" call, and all the monkeys will race for the center of the tree or dive to the ground. A "Snake!" call usually prompts the monkeys to stand still and look around before moving, to make sure that they do not run directly toward a crawling, unseen predator. Interestingly, this vervet vocabulary is not something the monkeys are born knowing. Youngsters need to learn these calls properly as they grow, and they often make mistakes.

Not surprisingly for animals that rely so much on their vision, monkeys are very sensitive to changes of expression on other's faces. The meanings of some expressions are obvious to any human observer. It is not hard to tell when a monkey is relaxed or angry. But humans can often mistake a nonhuman primate's meaning. A monkey pulling its lips back is not grinning but showing off its sharp, canine teeth—a warning to stay back. The gelada baboon goes so far as to turn its upper lip completely inside out to show off its teeth and gums. However, the gelada often raises its brow and pulls back its scalp at the same time to show off its striking white eyelids. No human observer has yet been able to say precisely what this signal means to another gelada.

Defenses

Although many monkeys are rather small animals, they are not easy prey for most predators. There are three reasons for this. First, because many monkeys live in trees, they are out of reach of most ground-prowling meat eaters. Second, because they live in groups, they all have very good alarm systems—lots of eyes and ears make sure that few predators can sneak up on them successfully. Third, that same group lifestyle means that monkeys can band together quickly to defend themselves, presenting any attacker with a gang rather than a single, vulnerable monkey.

For all tree dwellers—a category that includes all New World monkeys—the biggest danger comes from the biggest birds. The huge harpy eagle of South America, which may weigh as much as 20 pounds (9 kg), can successfully attack even a monkey as large as a 16-pound (7-kg) red howler. In Africa, the crowned hawk eagle and the martial eagle pose similar threats.

Still, monkeys living in the dense rain forest are fairly safe, unless they are caught exposed on outer branches. Monkeys living in more open forest are at greater risk. The savanna-dwelling monkeys, which spend most of their time on the ground, are the most vulnerable of all. Like vervets, baboons too are preyed upon by leopards and pythons, although they are not as easy to prey upon as one might expect. Baboons are big and strong, and males have very large and sharp canines. An angry group of snarling baboon males may present too big a risk, even for a leopard.

But baboons, like people, differ greatly in character. The safety of a baboon troop depends largely on the dominant males, and while some do not hesitate to face down a hungry cat, others will turn tail and run for cover. If they do, the smaller females and youngsters make easy targets.

There are a few other predators that monkeys must watch out for, and they are all fellow primates. Humans have traditionally been one of their major dangers. People throughout Africa and the Americas have long hunted monkeys for food. Chimpanzees also hunt monkeys; their favorites seem to be the red colobus and blue monkeys. Finally, some large monkey species occasionally hunt small monkeys. In Africa, baboons will at times feast on young vervets. In South America, capuchins will, if the opportunity presents itself, attack and kill squirrel monkeys.

To protect themselves, most monkeys have warning systems. While a baboon troop is foraging on the ground, for example, several older males usually guard the group by sitting atop high ground or termite mounds. Tree-dwelling monkeys, like-wise, usually have some members of the group on the fringes of the feeding area on the lookout for trouble. If they spot any, a loud and elaborate system of calls quickly warns the other monkeys to take shelter or run.

Some monkeys make use of other species to bolster their own warning systems. Vervets, for example, pay attention to the warning cries of birds that inhabit the same area they do. The birds, called superb starlings, also have different sounds that distinguish between predators on the ground and in the air, and the monkeys are able to translate them.

A number of monkey species make a point of traveling together with monkeys of a different species to give them added protection. They form what are called mixed-species groups, befriending and grooming the other monkeys as if they were members of their own group. Leaf-eating red colobus in West Africa, for example, often feed and travel with Diana monkeys. The Dianas are bigger than the red colobus and they are also better at catching sight of predatory chimpanzees.

Parenting

All mammals, from horses to humans, give their offspring a lot of attention. Mammal babies are completely dependent on their mothers for milk, and the first weeks of their lives are spent feeding and growing. One of the features that characterize primates is that they all have exceptionally long childhoods, so monkeys usually lavish much more care on their young than other mammals do.

Monkeys are born able to see the world around them and with the ability to hold on tightly to their mother's fur. They have to—most monkeys are born in trees and a tight grip is essential

A YOUNG BABOON BEGINS LIFE BY CLINGING TO ITS MOTHER'S CHEST; AFTER A FEW MONTHS, IT IS ABLE TO CLIMB ONTO HER BACK, AND IT WILL RIDE ON TOP OF HER UNTIL IT IS ABOUT A YEAR OLD..

for their survival. Most will cling to their mother constantly for the first month or two until they can begin to move around by themselves.

In many species, mothers get help in their parenting duties from other females in the group. Often these females are the infant's aunts or older sisters. In other cases, though, the babysitting monkeys are young females unrelated to the infant, but by taking care of another monkey's baby, they get valuable training in the skills they will need themselves someday.

Parenting chores are very different for the marmosets and tamarins of the Americas. Unlike all the other monkeys, which normally give birth to only one baby at a time, marmosets and tamarins routinely give birth to twins, and they often have two sets a year. Carrying around all those infants would be an exhausting job for a mother. So, among these monkeys, fathers play a leading parental role. After birth, the father carries the infants. The mother takes them only for feeding.

At times, tamarin and marmoset fathers will get help from other members from the group, most of which are the baby's aunts and uncles. Occasionally, an unrelated male that has joined the troop will also take over some child-care duties.

Throughout all monkey societies, babies generally receive a lot of attention, not just from their parents, but from the other troop members. Yet the attention they get is not always welcome. Babies are sometimes killed by males attempting to take control of the group. This happens among African baboons and blue monkeys, and is especially common among the Hanuman langurs of India. The males engage in this seemingly cruel practice because they are eager to produce offspring of their own, and the females cannot get pregnant as long as they are still feeding their young with milk. Feeding can go on for up to two years—too long for a male whose time at the top of the ladder might be brief.

The Mind of a Monkey

Monkeys are highly intelligent animals, but their intelligence is not the same as ours. It is something quite different, a fascinating mix of surprising abilities and, to most people, equally surprising limits.

Monkeys need a complex brain to keep track of everything that is going on in their group. They need to know who belongs and who does not, who is related to whom, who is higher in rank and who is lower, and which monkeys have special grooming relationships with one another. They also must be aware of every group member's distinctive personality. They have to keep in mind who desperately needs grooming and overtures of friendship, and who should be scrupulously avoided.

Many other mammals live in groups, of course. Wolves, for example, live in packs, in which certain wolves are dominant. All the other members of the pack are aware of their lower standing in relation to the pack leader. But a monkey knows not only its own standing in relation to a more or less dominant member of the group. It also knows the difference in rank between any other two members of the troop.

Some monkeys use that knowledge to form strong alliances when they need to. A bonnet macaque male, for example, when challenged by another member of the troop, will often seek out another male to help him defend himself against his rival. But the macaque does not choose the partner at random. Rather, he looks for a male that he knows outranks the monkey challenging him. The presence of the higher-ranking male often makes the challenger much less eager for confrontation.

Sometimes the ways in which monkeys use their social knowledge has an almost human—and not so pleasant—edge. Monkeys can squabble and fight among themselves as vehemently as any pack of human teenagers and they can, at times, be just as cruel. To answer an attack, monkeys do not always directly confront the attacker. They may instead respond by taking their revenge on a relative or friend of the other monkey even though this new victim has done nothing wrong.

THE TIGHT STRUCTURE OF BABOON SOCIETY SOMETIMES LEADS TO INTENSE COMPETITION AND FIGHTS BETWEEN MEMBERS OF A TROOP.

Another aspect of monkey intelligence has a more familiar feel to it. Some researchers think that monkeys have a nearly human ability to lie. Primatologists call this particular form of primate braininess Machiavellian intelligence, in honor of Niccolo Machiavelli, a famous Italian of the sixteenth century.

Machiavelli is best remembered today for a book he wrote called *The Prince*. It is filled with Machiavelli's advice to rulers of his day on the best techniques for governing their people. Those who hold power, Machiavelli wrote, should always appear to be honest and straightforward, and whenever possible, to actually be so. But, he advised, a ruler should always be ready to be dishonest if a lie will get him what he needs.

Monkeys, naturally, do not communicate with words and sentences as people do, so it is difficult to say that a monkey ever actually lies. But observers have certainly witnessed monkeys that appeared to be trying to deceive others. An example is given by a young baboon that scientists observed as it watched an adult female dig a tasty plant bulb out of the ground. The youngster quickly scanned the scene, saw no other baboons nearby, then suddenly screamed its lungs out in a way guaranteed to bring any primate mother running. The young baboon's mother, racing toward her child, saw the adult female near him and apparently concluded that her precious darling had been attacked. As the outraged mother charged, the puzzled and completely innocent female dropped the bulb and ran for safety. The bulb, of course, was casually picked up by the now calm and contented youngster.

Primatologists are divided over whether this baboon was truly attempting to deceive its mother. Did it actually plan to pretend that it had been attacked so it could get the food it wanted, or did it simply learn to associate its yelling with its getting the food? It is hard to tell the difference sometimes. However, this particular youngster was observed pulling the same trick several times, and each time, it screamed only when there were no other baboon witnesses around.

Pretending and deceiving—-and perhaps lying—are all methods humans use both to get what they want and to get along with other people around them. For example, we often tell people we like the food they have cooked, or the clothes they are wearing, even when we honestly do not, to avoid hurting their feelings. Or perhaps we might pretend not to like an item at a yard sale quite as much as we really do in an attempt to get it for a lower price. So it is easy to imagine that baboons and other monkeys have brains that work the same way ours do and that think the same kind of thoughts.

But here is another example of baboon behavior: in South Africa, baboons search for huge ostrich eggs, which they love. Yet when they find a nest of eggs, they do not seem to know exactly how to crack the eggs open. They pick one up and drop it. If it does not break, they pick it up and drop it again. They do this repeatedly, until the egg happens to hit another egg and crack. Then they delightedly lap up the contents. But they handle the next egg the same way they did the first. The baboons have learned that they need to perform the action of dropping the egg, but they do not seem to grasp the idea that the egg must hit something hard before it will break.

Other monkeys exhibit similar abilities and limitations. Capuchins, for example, are often said to be the smartest of the New World monkeys. They are the only ones that have learned to crack nuts by smashing them against tree trunks, and so, unlike baboons, they seem to understand not just the action, but also the idea behind it. In captivity, they have been taught to use simple tools, such as a stick, for pushing food out of a tube. But when the stick was exchanged for a string, they kept trying to use the string the same way they used the stick. Apparently, they are missing something in their understanding of what makes a particular tool suitable for a particular task.

Monkeys are undoubtedly very intelligent compared with other animals. Experiments have shown that they can count, at least to three, that they are good at mimicking the actions of others, and even at learning some surprisingly complex tasks. Rhesus macaques, for example, were able to learn how to use a computer joystick to play "shoot 'em up" video games. Like human children, they turned out to be naturally gifted at the games and quickly became competitive with each other. But completely unlike humans, no monkey can do something as simple as recognize itself in a mirror. In other words, monkeys may be very aware of the world around them but they are not aware of themselves in the same way we are. That ability is evidently beyond the power of the monkey's brain. Intriguingly, it is not beyond the power of the great apes. Chimpanzees, our closest cousins, can not only recognize themselves in a mirror but can also quickly learn to use a mirror to look behind them. No monkey in the world could ever do this.

5 Meet the Monkeys

T he roughly 200 species of monkeys spread across the globe display a wide range of sizes, colors, lifestyles, and behaviors—much too wide, in fact, to describe in detail in one brief book. A look at some of these creatures though, will at least hint at their fascinating diversity.

New World Monkeys

Marmosets and Tamarins

Several characteristics separate the thirty species that make up these two groups from all the others. Alone among the monkeys, marmosets and tamarins have claws, rather than nails, on all their fingers and toes, except on their big toes. With these long, sharp claws, they are better able to cling to tree trunks

WITH THEIR SHARP CLAWS, THIS FAMILY OF BARE-EARED MARMOSETS CAN HANG ON TIGHTLY TO THEIR TREE-BRANCH HOME IN THE BRAZILIAN RAIN FOREST.

while they bite into the wood with their front teeth—an activity they engage in frequently to get the sap and gum inside the tree to flow out. When not lapping up gum, these monkeys eat fruit and insects.

Marmosets are very small monkeys; the largest weighs only 10 ounces (300 g). In fact, in this group is the world's smallest monkey, the pygmy marmoset, which grows no bigger than 6 inches (15 cm) and weighs no more than 4.9 ounces (140 g). Tamarins tend to be a little larger than marmosets. But even the biggest tips the scales at just 20 ounces (585 g).

Both types of monkeys live in small family groups that tend to put a lot of child rearing and carrying responsibility on the fathers. Tamarins and marmosets differ chiefly in where they live. Tamarins live on the northwest side of the Amazon River. Marmosets live mainly on the southeast side. Between them though, they cover a broad section of South America, stretching from the Pacific to the Atlantic oceans.

Howlers

Howlers are large tree-dwelling monkeys, with males weighing up to 25 pounds (11.5 kg). Unfortunately, this makes them prime targets for human hunters. But their size protects the adults at least from most other predators, except for the very largest eagles.

There are six species of howler monkeys and they move through the forests of the Americas from southern Mexico all the way down to northern Argentina. None of them moves quickly though. Howlers are slow, deliberate leaf eaters, and they spend most of their day simply sitting around and digesting their large bellyful of leaves. While at rest, they use their strong prehensile tails to tie them firmly to a tree branch. When they do move, they walk leisurely on all fours, or swing slowly, arm over arm, through the branches. They almost never leap from tree to tree.

EVEN MONKEYS CAN FALL FROM TREES. RED HOWLERS, WHICH ARE AMONG THE LARGEST MONKEYS OF THE AMERICAS, ANCHOR THEMSELVES WITH THEIR PREHENSILE TAILS TO BE SAFE.

As a group, the howlers' main claim to fame, and the talent that gives them their name, is their shockingly loud vocal ability. Howler calls can be heard for miles, and since they often call at dawn, howlers serve as the roosters of the rain forest. The primary purpose of the group's loud howling—actually, more of a roaring—is to keep other troops of howlers away from their territory. Occasionally, howler troops meet, with each attempting to claim the same patch of forest. When this happens, the battle between them rages, but usually only vocally. The contending

A CAPUCHIN MAY BE NEAT WHEN PICKING SMALL FRUIT, BUT WHEN HUNTING FOR INSECTS IT MAY GO ON A MESSY, DESTRUCTIVE RAMPAGE, RIPPING THE BARK RIGHT OFF OF TREES.

troops both start howling for all they are worth. Every once in a while, these contests will end in a physical struggle, but most often the louder, more persistent group wins, without any actual fighting taking place.

Capuchins and Squirrel Monkeys

A century or so ago, the organ grinder was a common sight on city streets: a man who would turn the crank on a mechanical music box while a costumed monkey would collect coins from onlookers. Most often that monkey was a capuchin, considered by many to be among the smartest monkeys and among the most easily trained. Also making them valuable for this profession was their toughness—capuchins can live a long time in captivity, with some of them reaching ages of forty-five or fifty.

Capuchins are strong, somewhat chunky monkeys with the biggest males about 22 inches (56 cm) long and weighing about 8 to 9 pounds (4 kg). They are also among the messiest monkeys when eating. As a troop of capuchins move through the top of the forest, they rip apart nearly everything in their quest for food. Although their preferred food is fruit, they need to eat a fair number of insects or other animals to get enough protein in their diet. They use their strong hands and jaws to rip the bark off trees, looking for any insects or spiders lurking beneath it. They will also grab snails and tree frogs, and on occasion, a small squirrel monkey.

Despite that infrequent danger, squirrel monkeys and capuchins often feed together. Both types are among the most widespread of the New World monkeys and are found throughout Central and South America. Squirrel monkeys are considerably smaller and more slender than capuchins, usually growing no bigger than 14 inches (35 cm) and weighing no more than 2.6 pounds (1.2 kg).

Its intelligence, small size, and attractive face once made the squirrel monkey popular as a pet, but not for long—away from the forest most monkeys do not survive.

Squirrel monkeys are probably what most people picture when asked to call an image of a monkey to mind. With their gray heads and muzzles and their white-masked faces, squirrel monkeys look like the sock puppets of the forest. Because these monkeys are rather small, they band together in large groups for added protection. Often they travel in troops of 40 or more and sometimes they come together in "herds" of 400 or even 500 individuals. Such numbers keep the squirrel monkeys safe, not only from predators, but also from the bullying of larger monkeys that might try to push them aside from desirable food.

Like the capuchins, squirrel monkeys are primarily fruit and flower eaters, but they too eat a lot of insects. Sometimes it seems they prefer insects to any other food. Although they do not have the strength to rip apart tree bark as their larger cousins do, they are very good at finding and grabbing multitudes of caterpillars and grasshopper larvae, along with any other insects crawling on the branches. Squirrel monkeys also take advantage of the capuchins' messy manners. In Central America strong capuchins have learned to open tough palm nuts by cracking them against the trees. In these same forests, squirrel monkeys have learned to hang out in the tree branches below the capuchins, catching all the bits that the larger monkeys drop.

Spider Monkeys

Spider monkeys are about the same size and weight as the howlers. But these fruit eaters are far more active and acrobatic than the slow, careful howlers. With their long arms and flexible shoulders, spider monkeys swing easily from branch to branch. They also do not hesitate to make spectacular leaps between trees, throwing out their arms and legs widely to catch hold of twigs and leaves when they land. Finally, spider monkeys have very strong prehensile tails that can support their full weight. Hanging from a branch by its tail, a spider monkey can

A SPIDER MONKEY COMES CLOSEST TO THE IMAGE MOST PEOPLE HAVE OF MONKEYS AS ACROBATS. IT HAS LONG ARMS FOR SWINGING AND CAN HANG FROM ITS TAIL ALONE.

pick otherwise unreachable fruit or drink from a pond below, without ever coming down from the tree.

The one physical feature spider monkeys cannot boast about are thumbs. Thumbs, though generally handy items to have, are a hindrance when swinging quickly, and over the course of evolution, spider monkeys have gradually lost them.

Spider monkeys are closely related to the woolly monkeys, which lead similar lives but have slightly bigger bodies and dense, thick fur. Bigger than them all is the muriqui, or the woolly spider monkey, which grows 30 inches (76 cm) from head to toe and is probably the biggest of New World monkeys.

Old World Monkeys

Guenons

The guenons are a big group of Old World monkeys made up of some two dozen species. Among them they cover nearly all of Africa below the inhospitable Sahara. Most of the guenons are medium-sized monkeys, but not all. One species, the talapoin, is the smallest of all the Old World monkeys; it weighs a mere 1.5 pounds (.7 kg). At the other extreme is the 22-pound (10-kg) patas monkey. Among the few features the guenons share is that they all have cheek pouches, which allow them to shovel a lot of food into their mouths quickly while foraging and then enjoy it later at their leisure.

Mostly, what they prefer to stuff their cheeks with is fruit, but like all fruit eaters, they must add other nutrients to their meals. The smaller guenons depend on insects for this purpose; the larger ones eat leaves. Often several different guenon species feed in the same area at the same time, but they usually do not directly compete with one another. They stay out of each other's way by feeding at different levels in the forest, with some higher up in the trees and some lower, or by selecting different foods.

Although they may hang out together, the various guenons have no trouble distinguishing their own species from all the others. The guenons are clothed in an unusually rich display of fur color and facial markings, and some of them are the most visually striking of all monkeys. Among them is the beautiful Diana monkey of West Africa, a gray-black monkey decked out in a long white cape of fur with white stripes along its thighs and hips. Another is De Brazza's monkey, which has a black face framed by an orange crown rising from its forehead and a long white beard descending from its jaw.

One of the most impressive of the guenons, the patas monkey, is not really very typical of the group. Although the patas

MANY SPECIES OF AFRICAN GUENONS, SUCH AS THIS DE BRAZZA'S MONKEY, HAVE VERY DISTINCTIVE FACIAL MARKINGS, A TRAIT THAT MAY HELP THE MONKEYS PICK EACH OTHER OUT IN A CROWD.

monkey shares the guenons' usual good looks—male patas have a white moustache and a regal mane of white fur on their shoulders—they do not share their fondness for forests. Patas monkeys prefer open grasslands, and they spend most of their daytime hours on the ground.

Patas monkeys are the only monkeys really built for running. They have long, equal-length arms and legs, and when they need to they can get their limbs moving quickly. Patas monkeys can race through the African savanna effortlessly, hitting speeds of 35 miles per hour (58 kph).

That speed is often essential for their survival. The patas are preyed on by jackals, hyenas, and leopards, among other meat eaters, and away from any sheltering trees they rely on running their way out of danger. Patas society is organized around the need for security. A troop of twenty to thirty monkeys is generally composed of females and youngsters, with a single dominant adult male. The male, though, is not so much the general of the troop as he is its vigilant sentry. Leadership is left to the dominant females. The male's duty is to be on guard constantly for any danger. Should a predator appear, he will quickly divert its attention by showing himself boldly on top of high ground or by running in the wrong direction, away from the troop. The other monkeys, meanwhile, race to safety.

Because of the patas' preference for grassland, they often run into farms that people have carved out of the savanna. Their speed and stealth make them excellent crop raiders, which means that human farmers are also among the patas monkey's major predators.

Baboons and Geladas

Baboons are easily the most widespread of the African monkeys. They have put down roots nearly all over the continent south of the Sahara, living successfully in many different habitats, from the Namibian Desert in the north to the cool mountains of South Africa and the humid grasslands in the east and the west.

Unlike most other monkeys, baboons have a prominent snout and a four-legged stance that makes them appear nearly doglike. They are some of the largest monkeys, and males can weigh as much as 90 to 100 pounds (41 to 46 kg). Female baboons are much smaller, usually only half the size of males. Baboons are also very strong and built for living on the ground. Their arms are proportionately much longer than other monkeys', so when they walk their shoulders are held high. So is their head, which allows them to scan the land around them for danger without rising on two legs. Their hands are much like human hands and are very good for digging up roots and bulbs. Their feet, meanwhile, are rather flatter than other monkeys' feet. Those flat feet give baboons more stability on the ground but they are not as good at curling around branches, so baboons are not great tree climbers. Still, at night they pull themselves up into the trees to sleep.

Because baboons are big animals, they need a lot of food. Consequently, they spend a large portion of every day searching for things to eat. Fortunately, they will eat nearly anything. Fruit is their favorite food, as it is for most monkeys. But baboons will happily devour grass, seeds, roots, and bulbs, along with eggs, lizards, shellfish, birds, and small mammals, including an occasional monkey or young antelope.

Baboon societies are highly organized, and the members are all keenly aware of the strict hierarchy. Troops of forty to eighty baboons move across the savanna with the strongest, most dominant males in front and younger, less dominant males in the rear and along the sides to protect youngsters and females from attack.

Scientists have studied baboons extensively. Partly this is because these large monkeys, being ground dwellers, are easier

THE HAMADRYAS BABOON LIVES FARTHER NORTH THAN THE OTHER BABOONS AND WAS ONCE COMMON THROUGHOUT EGYPT. THIS IS THE TYPE OF BABOON DEPICTED IN ANCIENT EGYPTIAN ART.

to follow than are their cousins high in the trees. But it is also because baboon society is so complex and fascinating. Baboon troops do not change much over time. Females seldom leave; younger males often stay with the troop also (although both males and females may leave if the group gets too large). As a result, researchers can spend years following the fortunes of a single group of baboons, noting the distinct personalities, the

A BABOON'S LONG, SHARP CANINE TEETH ARE POWERFUL WEAPONS, AND THEIR DISPLAY IS NOT AN EMPTY THREAT.

tensions between rivals, their individual ambitions and fears. They can track which males are eager for dominance, which females are most protective of their babies, and which members will form alliances as a new generation grows up and tries to take over. At times, observing baboons, even the most objective scientist has trouble not thinking of them in human terms.

Primatologists disagree on how many species of baboons exist. Some group them all as one species, while others see five separate ones (yellow, anubis, guinea, chacma, and hamadryas). But all agree that the gelada baboon is quite different and in a category of its own.

Geladas live only in the grasslands that lie high on the mountains of Ethiopia. They are dedicated grass eaters, so much so that they have developed a unique feeding posture. Sitting straight up on the ground, they use their hands to harvest all the grass within reach. Then, without getting up, they shuffle forward on their bottoms to get to the next patch of grass.

Geladas are so specialized to their habitat that they find it difficult to climb trees. At night they sleep on rocky outcrops or steep cliffs to keep them safe from predators.

Macaques

When it comes to toughness, the macaques outdo all the other monkeys. They represent some twenty species, spread across India, Afghanistan, Pakistan, China, and the nations of Southeast Asia, north into the islands of Japan, and south into the Philippines and Malaysia. They also occupy the rocky outposts of North Africa and the European island of Gibraltar. In their range, they have accommodated themselves to every available habitat, from rain forest to mountain. They have also thrived alongside humans, in cities and on farms.

A few macaque species stand out as especially tough, stubborn survivors. The Barbary macaque has made a home in the harsh Atlas Mountains of Morocco, where it lives in evergreen forests year-round. During the winter, these forests are often buried in snow, and the monkeys get by on a diet of cedar needles and bark. The same species forms the macaque population on Gibraltar and is Europe's only resident wild monkey.

Beating even them for fortitude may be the Japanese macaques, some of which live high in the mountains on the island of Honshu, where winter temperatures may fall to 5 degrees F (-15 degrees C). Snowfalls here can be heavy. Yet the monkeys do not seem to be bothered. They are protected by the very thick fur they grow in winter, a coat that makes them seem almost bearlike. They have also developed the habit of taking mid-winter baths in natural hot springs that dot the mountains.

However, the toughest macaque of all may be the rhesus macaque. Some macaques, such as the bonnet macaque, are known for being easygoing and peaceful. Rhesus macaques are nothing like that. They are fierce and aggressive when disturbed, and they live in a tense society of dominant males and females. These are hardy, medium-sized monkeys with males weighing in at around 17 pounds (7.7 kg) and brandishing razor-sharp, large canines. They live in a broad swath of southern Asia and can deal with temperatures from 104 degrees F (40 degrees C) in tropical forests to -4 degrees F (-20 degrees C) in mountain homes 13,000 feet (4,000 m) above sea level.

They can also adapt easily to humans. In parts of India, where religious restrictions help ensure the monkeys' safety, more than half of rhesus macaques live in contact with humans. They have invaded farms, villages, and towns, and they have taken up residence in train stations and in temples. Like baboons, these macaques will eat nearly anything. Among their favorite foods are clovers and herbs, but the constant presence of tourists and worshippers has gotten them used to a diet that ranges from fried bread to ice cream.

In the United States and in Europe, rhesus macaques have also become used to humans, but most of these humans are scientists. These macaques have the doubtful distinction of being the most widely used monkeys in medical research laboratories.

MANY PEOPLE THINK THAT THE ASIAN DOUC LANGUR, SHOWN HERE NURSING AN INFANT, IS ONE OF THE MOST BEAUTIFUL OF ALL MONKEYS.

Colobus, Proboscis, and Langurs

The colobus monkeys make up a collection of nine species of leaf eaters that stretch right across the middle of Africa. They do not stick rigidly to the single food item. They also eat fruit, flowers, twigs, and seeds. But leaves are their main meal. Most spend their entire lives in the trees, although some do come down to the ground occasionally to eat soil—apparently the dirt provides them with minerals that their otherwise leafy diet does

BOTH MALE AND FEMALE PROBOSCIS MONKEYS ARE MARKED BY ODD NOSES, ALTHOUGH THE FEMALE'S IS TURNED UP RATHER THAN DOWN. A YOUNG PROBOSCIS HAS A BLUE NOSE; IT TURNS PINK AS THE MONKEY MATURES.

not. Red colobus monkeys on the island of Zanzibar sometimes eat lumps of charcoal, which may help their digestive system handle natural poisons present in the leaves they eat.

Colobus monkeys have big stomachs—leaves are not easy to digest and these monkeys spend a lot of time resting while their bodies devote their energy to turning leaves into usable fuel. Among the leaf eaters are the black-and-white colobus monkeys, famed for the fine white fur that fringes their black face like a halo and hangs down from their arms.

In Asia a much bigger and related group of leaf-eating monkeys are the langurs. Except for the Hanuman langur of India (named for the Hindu god), the twenty-nine species of langurs also spend their whole lives in the trees, surrounded by their food supply. (The Hanuman langur often lives in mountainous areas as well as around cities, and sleeps on the sides of steep cliffs.) Among the Asian langurs are a number of visually striking monkeys including both some of the oddest looking and some of the most beautiful.

The proboscis monkeys are in that first category. Proboscis males have huge trunklike noses that hang down over their lips. To humans these outside appendages make the monkeys look comic. To some observers the forest dwellers they resemble most are Snow White's cartoon companions. The nose can be so long that the monkey has to push it aside in order to eat. Female proboscis monkeys, however, which have smaller upturned noses, apparently find the biggest-nosed males to be the most attractive.

Proboscis monkeys live only in the swampy mangrove forests on the island of Borneo in Indonesia. In that habitat they often display their skill as swimmers. They are among the minority of monkeys that not only swim but swim well, both on the surface and underwater.

The proboscises' opposite may be the snub-nosed monkeys of China, some of which live high up in evergreen mountain forests. One of the little-nosed species, the Yunnan snub-nosed monkey, is the world's highest-living monkey, making its home in snowy forests 12,700 feet (4,100 m) above sea level.

6 Monkeys and Humans

Although monkeys are our evolutionary cousins, we humans have rarely treated them with care and respect. For the most part we have made use of them for our own purposes and almost never to the monkeys' benefit. In general, people have long viewed monkeys as good for only three things: for use as food, as pets, and as research subjects.

Throughout Central and South America, Africa, and most parts of Asia, people have always hunted monkeys. The hunt continues to this day. In the past, the hunting was done by individuals or small groups seeking only enough meat to feed their family or tribe. Hunting like this kills relatively few monkeys and does not seriously harm the monkey population as a whole. Today, however, much of the hunting is to provide meat not for traditional forest-dwelling people but to meet a growing demand for monkey flesh among city dwellers throughout the tropics. The problem is especially severe in West Africa but it poses a serious threat to monkeys wherever they live in the world. This so-called bushmeat trade is having a very serious

MANDRILLS ARE THE WORLD'S LARGEST MONKEYS, WITH MALES AVERAGING 70 POUNDS (32 KG) AND SOME WEIGHING MORE THAN 100 POUNDS (45 KG). THEY HAVE BEEN HUNTED SO HEAVILY THAT THEY ARE NOW ENDANGERED.

EVERY YEAR, HUNTERS KILL MILLIONS OF MONKEYS TO SUPPLY CITY DWELLERS WITH MEAT. THE SLAUGHTER IS HELPING TO PUSH MANY SPECIES TOWARD EXTINCTION.

impact on many monkey species, particularly the larger monkeys. In Africa, the large, baboonlike drills of the rain forest have been hunted to the brink of extinction. In South America, people eat millions of monkeys every year, and hunting for monkey meat is threatening such groups as capuchins, woolly monkeys, howler monkeys, and spider monkeys. Their size makes them more valuable and the pursuit more economical.

In seeing monkeys as little more than convenient sources of meat, people have treated their primate relatives no differently than other animals. The same attitude has led to the use of monkey skin and fur for a variety of luxury clothing and furnishings. The beautiful black-and-white colobus monkeys of Africa proved especially desirable to fashion-conscious Europeans in the late nineteenth century. Between 1880 and 1900, to meet a demand for black-and-white monkey-fur coats, more than 2.5

IN THE PAST, TASTES IN HUMAN FASHION PROVED DANGEROUS TO THE BLACK-AND-WHITE COLOBUS MONKEY, WHOSE BEAUTIFUL, LONG FUR WAS TURNED INTO TRENDY COATS AND RUGS.

million of these monkeys were killed. The slaughter did not end with the turn of the century. Over the next decades, more multitudes of black-and-white colobus were killed to make striking small rugs.

Monkey Pests

Many more monkeys have been killed by people who regarded them as troublesome raiders of crops. In some cases, the human complaints are undoubtedly justified. Monkeys are clever and curious and they are often open to trying new foods. Like crows, bears, foxes, rats, and so many other animals, monkeys will certainly take advantage of easily obtainable food whenever possible. For small farmers in Africa and Asia, the amount of destruction a troop of monkeys can inflict is quite significant. Usually the culprits are the smartest, most adaptable monkeys: baboons in Africa, macaques in Asia.

In nearly all cases, the development of a monkey pest is the result of humans moving into territory that had been the monkeys' domain. In some spots, though, people have managed to create a monkey problem where no monkeys originally existed. This has often happened on islands that had always been kept monkey-free by the great expanses of ocean that separated them from continental forests.

On the island of Mauritius in the Indian Ocean, for example, six Asian macaques were let loose by European sailors sometime in the early 1700s. Those half dozen have now grown to a substantial population of more than 30,000, and they are more than a minor nuisance to farmers.

Imported macaques caused similar problems far away in Puerto Rico. Other Caribbean islands, such as Barbados and

St. Kitts, have become home to great hordes of African vervets, which devastate not only the human farms but also the food supply of many animals native to the island.

Welcome Guests

Despite their hostile reception by people in many parts of the world, in a few places monkeys are tolerated, and even indulged. Throughout India, Hindus consider Hanuman langurs sacred animals and feed them rather than hunt them. The large gray monkeys can often be seen in groups around Hindu temples, especially where they are likely to be fed by tourists. But they are a constant presence in many towns and cities, pestering people for food and raiding shops.

A number of monkeys have religion to thank for whatever protection they might enjoy. Buddhists, for example, attach special significance to Japanese macaques. Muslims, although they do not consider the animal sacred, are prohibited from eating monkey flesh. So in many Muslim countries hunting for food, at least, is not a big threat to local monkey populations.

Monkey Helpers

Unlike dogs or horses, monkeys have never really been domesticated by humans and put to work. But there are a few examples of monkeys being trained for service as human helpers.

In Malaysia, macaques are employed as coconut pickers. The monkeys are far better than humans at climbing the tall palm trees and can get to the coconuts at the top quickly. Once there, they pick off all the ripe coconuts and drop them to the ground.

MONKEYS GENERALLY DO NOT FARE WELL IN HUMAN HOMES, BUT A SMALL NUMBER HAVE BEEN TRAINED SUCCESSFULLY TO SERVE AS HELPERS FOR PARALYZED PEOPLE.

Capuchins have also found employment. Some have been trained to act as assistants for people who have been paralyzed. These very intelligent monkeys have learned to carry objects, take food out of a refrigerator, put food in a microwave oven, and pick up a ringing telephone.

Other Uses for a Live Monkey

Monkeys as workers are rare. A much more common use for a live monkey is as a pet. People who live in the tropics have always taken some monkeys to live with them, as pets for themselves or their intrigued children. Among South American peoples, marmosets and tamarins are common as pets. There have been periods when fads for monkey pets swept through nontropical cultures as well. Several hundred years ago a monkey was a status symbol eagerly collected by European princes and nobles. For a few decades after the Second World War, squirrel monkeys became familiar pets in the United States.

Monkeys, though, require an enormous amount of care to make sure that they do not get ill. Because monkeys are vulnerable to most of the same diseases that humans get, the great majority of monkey pets die at a young age. The few that survive become a huge burden on owners who try to keep them healthy and happy.

Monkeys and Medicine

The same vulnerability that makes monkeys problematic pets, however, makes them good subjects for medical research. Because the monkey body is so similar to our own, scientists developing new drugs and vaccines have found that they could test their efforts on monkeys before trying them out on people.

This knowledge grew slowly during the twentieth century. Researchers first discovered in 1908 that monkeys could be infected with polio, a terrible disease that, if it did not kill its human victims, often left them paralyzed. Within a few years, researchers found that monkeys could also be infected with measles, mumps, and yellow fever.

At the time, however, medical researchers in Europe and in the United States could not do very much with that knowledge. The reason was simple: they could not get their hands on enough monkeys to use in their laboratories. Monkeys had to be carried from their tropical homes by boat, and many died during the long trip. In the late 1940s the increasing use of airplanes

No monkey species has proved more valuable to medical research than the rhesus macaque; its use has led to many vaccines and treatments for devastating human diseases.

changed all that. Scientists began shipping monkeys by the thousands for experiments that might lead to treatments or cures for a host of diseases.

The monkey species they favored was the rhesus macaque. These monkeys were very adaptable, accustomed to living near humans, and could tolerate cool climates. They were also very well known to scientists. Research on these monkeys led to the discovery of a substance all humans carry in their blood called the Rh factor. There are two types of Rh factor, and people are described as being either Rh positive or Rh negative. Either type is fine. Problems arise only when a woman of one type becomes pregnant with a baby of a different type. The mother's immune system then attacks the "invader" inside her, either killing the baby or damaging its brain. The discovery of the Rh factor in rhesus macaques—the name of the substance comes from the "rh" in *rhesus*—allowed scientists to develop a vaccine to prevent the problem from occurring.

In the 1950s an epidemic of polio cases in the United States pushed American scientists to search desperately for a vaccine against this devastating disease. Laboratories began importing rhesus macaques by the hundreds of thousands.

No one knows precisely how many monkeys died in the search for a polio vaccine. The lowest estimate is around 100,000. Other estimates range from one million to as many as 5 million. But we do know how many human lives were saved. Before the first vaccine was ready for public use in 1955, some 20,000 Americans died or were paralyzed by polio every year. By the early 1960s, polio had virtually disappeared in the United States.

Since then, monkeys have been used in the development of many medical treatments, including the vaccines against rubella (German measles) and hepatitis B, drugs used to fight mental illness and cancer, surgical techniques and medicines necessary for organ transplants, and the development of contact lenses. In addition, research on monkey brains has yielded insights that may one day help doctors treat such destructive brain and nervous system disorders as strokes, Alzheimer's disease, and Parkinson's disease.

Clearly the contribution of these monkeys to our prospects for healthier lives has been extremely valuable. But it comes at the price of these animals' lives—and it takes a lot of animals. Many people, however saddened they may be by the monkeys' sacrifice, believe it is worth it if the result is the saving of human lives. Many others, however, have doubts. They question whether people have the right to kill our fellow primates—intelligent, sensitive animals like ourselves—just for our own benefit.

The debate over whether we should use monkeys for scientific research began to intensify during the 1960s and it continues to this day. There are seriously concerned people on both sides of the issue, and it is unlikely that the question will ever be resolved to everyone's satisfaction. But the debate has at least caused many changes in the ways humans use monkeys.

Medical researchers were not the only ones to exploit monkeys. The military did also, seeing how monkeys fared when exposed to a variety of gunshot wounds. They also exposed monkeys to atomic bomb tests, high levels of radiation, and a host of deadly bacteria- and virus-based weapons. Finally, beginning in the late 1940s, they used monkeys to test rockets and space capsules before sending any humans into space.

Some of the most intense criticism of scientists' attitudes toward monkeys was directed at experiments carried out by psychologists curious to see the effects of extreme conditions on a monkey's mental state. In the worst of these experiments, monkey infants were taken away from their mothers, placed in cages too small for them to move in, or isolated for years without being able to even see another monkey, let alone physically interact with it. The intent of such experiments was to gain knowledge about how such conditions lead to severe mental and emotional problems in humans. But critics, including many scientists, found such disregard for the monkeys horrifying.

IN THE 1950S AND EARLY 1960S, THE UNITED STATES EMPLOYED MONKEYS AS SUBSTITUTES FOR HUMAN ASTRONAUTS IN TESTS OF ROCKET SAFETY. THIRTY-TWO MONKEYS ACTUALLY FLEW IN SPACE.

Today, all universities and the federal government have strict guidelines that determine what kind of experiments may be performed on primates. They also specify the conditions in which monkeys must be kept. People have come to understand that monkeys need the company of one another as much as they need air and water. The result is that monkeys slated for experimentation are at least kept in an environment that allows them to be as healthy and happy as possible for as long as possible.

Scientists in the United States still use around 50,000 monkeys a year for research. But they no longer take monkeys from the wild for use in laboratories. Instead the monkeys are born and raised in primate research facilities around the country. That in itself is a significant change in the monkeys' prospects for the future. By some estimates, between the 1950s and 1970s, the number of rhesus macaques in India shrank by 90 percent as millions of the monkeys were shipped off to labs in the United States and Europe.

The Monkeys' Future

By making it illegal to bring monkeys into the United States, the government has helped to lesson the threat to monkey populations around the world. Many other countries have done likewise. And many nations where monkeys are found have passed laws against hunting or selling them. Yet many monkey species are in serious danger of disappearing.

Part of the problem stems from the fact that not all the laws protecting monkeys can be enforced. In South America, Africa, and Asia many monkeys are still killed by hunters, even in those countries where to do so is against the law.

However, the biggest threat to monkeys comes from the loss of their forest home. Forests everywhere are disappearing from the Earth. Some go as their valuable trees are cut down for wood and paper. Others vanish as people clear the land for farms, ranches, or homes. Nowhere is the destruction more rapid than in precisely those areas where the greatest number of monkeys dwell.

Monkeys suffer in several ways from the destruction. First, of course, they lose the trees they need for shelter and food. Second, the roads people build through the forest—either to connect farms to towns and cities or to allow logging trucks to carry the trees to market—make it easier for hunters to reach areas of the forest that were previously too hard to get to. Third, by erecting farms and towns in the monkeys' midst, people encourage the monkeys to raid crops, stores, and homes for food. That activity naturally allows people to then see the monkeys as pests and to feel justified in killing them.

All this is taking a tremendous toll on monkeys around the world. At least forty-nine monkey species, approximately one-quarter of the total, are considered to be in danger of extinction in the near future. It is not just monkeys that are in danger—apes are threatened even more, and orangutans, gorillas, and chimps are all in trouble. Many non-primates are suffering too, of course, from pandas to polar bears, along with an army of birds, fish, and even insects and spiders. Somehow, though, it seems especially painful to think of so many of our near relatives disappearing from our planet. Primates are resourceful, adaptable animals, and for a long time people could take some comfort in the knowledge that no primate species we know of has gone extinct in the past 200 years. But that may be about to change.

During the first years of the twenty-first century, scientists have mounted a search for a monkey called Miss Waldron's red colobus. The last time anyone definitely saw one of these leaf-eating African monkeys was in 1978, and scientists fear that the species may now be extinct. If so, it may merely be the first in a parade of extinctions unless people find ways to stop the destruction of the monkeys' world.

Glossary

adapids—cat-sized, tree-dwelling mammals that appeared some 55 million years ago and were the first "true" primates

adapt—to change in a way that allows an organism to function better in a new or different environment

anthropoids—the group of primates that includes monkeys, apes, and humans

carnivore—an animal that eats other animals

class—a level of biological classification above order and below phylum; all members of the order of Primates, for example, belong to the class Mammalia, or mammals

climate—the average kind of weather in a particular region over a long time

descendants—all of an animal's offspring: its children, grandchildren, great grandchildren, great great grandchildren, and so on

dominant—controlling or ruling over others; the dominant animals in a group command the attention of all the others

evolve—to change over time; species evolve over many thousands and millions of years

extinct—gone forever; a plant or animal is extinct when there is not a single one of its kind alive anywhere in the world

family—a level of classification above genus and below order; the different genera of New World monkeys are assigned to two families, Old World monkeys to one

fossil—the remains of an animal or plant that lived thousands or millions of years ago

genus—a level of classification above species and below family; the many species of guenons, for instance, all belong to the genus *Cercopithecus*

groom—in monkeys, to comb through the fur of another monkey, picking out bits of food, dead skin, or insects

gum—a soft, sticky substance in trees that flows to and seals off any injury

habitat—the kind of environment in which a plant or animal normally lives and grows

immune system—made up of the cells in an organism that recognize and attempt to destroy foreign cells or organisms

kingdom—the highest level of classification, such as Plantae (plants) or Animalia (animals)

mammal—a member of the class (Mammalia) of animals that routinely have hair or fur, and in which females give birth to live young and nourish those young with milk

nocturnal—active at night

omnivore—an animal that eats nearly everything, including both plants and meat

organism—an individual living thing; a single plant or animal

paleontologist—a scientist who studies fossils to learn about the life of the past

plesiadapids—small, nocturnal, tree-dwelling mammals that were the earliest ancestors of primates

predator—an animal that hunts and eats other animals

prehensile—able to grasp things; a prehensile tail can wrap around and tightly grip a branch

prey—an animal that is hunted by a predator

Primates—the order of mammals that includes prosimians, monkeys, and apes, including humans

primatologist—a scientist who specializes in the study of primates

prosimians—the group of small, nocturnal, tree-dwelling primates that includes lemurs, lorises, and tarsiers

savanna—generally flat, tropical grasslands broken up by occasional clumps of trees

sexual dimorphism—the existence of different body forms or sizes for males and females of a single species

species—the basic unit of classification that defines a "specific" type of animal or plant; all humans belong to the single species *Homo sapiens* while monkeys belong to some 200 different species

temperate—describes a climate with a moderate range of temperatures, cooler and more seasonal than the tropics

tropics—those regions of Earth directly above and below the equator, where the climate is generally hot and humid

GENUS CHECKLIST

Monkey Classification

Monkeys are generally divided into two groups, the New World monkeys of Central and South America, and the Old World monkeys of Africa and Asia. The New World monkeys are then further divided into two families. The first contains the marmosets and tamarins; the second contains all the others. All the Old World monkeys are put into a single family. Each family is then divided into a number of genera (singular, genus), and each genus is divided into individual species. Scientists do not all agree on precisely how many species of monkey exist (some consider particular kinds of monkeys to be separate species, others think they are different varieties of a single species), but there are roughly 200. Here are the groups to which they belong:

NEW WORLD MONKEYS

Cebidae	Lagothrix	woolly monkeys
	Ateles	spider monkeys
	Brachyteles	muriqui, or woolly spider monkey
	Alouatta	howler monkeys
	Pithecia	sakis
	Chiropotes	bearded sakis
	Cacajao	uakaris
	Callicebus	titi monkeys
	Aotus	night monkeys
	Cebus	capuchins
	Saimiri	squirrel monkeys
Callitrichidae	Callimico	Goeldi's monkey
	Saguinus	tamarins
	Callithrix	marmosets
	Cebuella	pygmy marmosets
	Leontopithecus	lion tamarins

OLD WORLD MONKEYS

	Erythrocebus	patas monkey
	Chlorocebus	savanna guenons (includes vervets and green monkeys)
	Cercopithecus	guenons (includes De Brazza's monkey, blue monkeys, Diana monkey)
	Miopithecus	talapoins
	Allenopithecus	Allen's swamp monkey
	Cercocebus	mangabeys
	Lophocebus	black mangabeys
	Macaca	Macaques (includes Barbary, bonnet, Japanese, long-tailed, and rhesus macaques)
	Papio	Baboons (includes chacma, hamadryas, yellow, anubis, and guinea baboons
	Mandrillus	mandrills and drills
	Theropithecus	gelada baboons
	Nasalis	proboscis monkeys
	Simias	pig-tailed monkeys
	Pygathrix	douc langur
	Rhinopithecus	snub-nosed monkeys
	Presbytis	langurs
	Semnopithecus	Hanuman langur
	Trachypithecus	capped langur
	Colobus	black and white colobus
	Piliocolobus	red colobus
	Procolobus	olive colobus

Further Research

Books for Young People

Knight, Tim. *Journey into the Rainforest*. New York: Oxford University Press, 2001.

Mathews, Tom L. *Light Shining Through the Mist: A Photobiography of Dian Fossey*. Washington, D.C.: National Geographic Society, 1998.

Powzyk, Joyce A. *In Search of Lemurs: My Days and Nights in a Madagascar Rain Forest*. Washington, D.C.: National Geographic Society, 1998.

Redmond, Ian. *Gorilla, Monkey & Ape*. New York: DK Publishing, 2000.

Swan, Erin *Primates: From Howler Monkeys to Humans*. Danbury, CT: Franklin Watts, 1999.

Web Sites

http://nationalzoo.si.edu/Animals/Primates/ForKids/
>	This is the site of the Smithsonian's National Zoo in Washington, D.C.
>	Click on the "Meet the Primates" link for info about howlers,
>	marmosets, tamarins, and some non-monkey relatives.

http://pin.primate.wisc.edu/factsheets/
>	Detailed information about individual primate species, together with
>	photos and lots of links for each animal, from the National Primate
>	Research Center at the University of Wisconsin-Madison.

http://www.virtualexplorers.org/ghana/monkey.htm

In 2001 wildlife biologist Lindsay Magnuson went into the forests of Ghana to investigate the lives of rolaway monkeys, aka Diana guenons. This site lets you accompany her on a virtual field trip.

Bibliography

Berger, Gotthart. *Monkeys and Apes*. New York: Arco Publishing, 1985.

Blum, Deborah. *The Monkey Wars*. New York: Oxford University Press, 1994.

Byrne, Richard W. and Andrew Whitten, eds. *Machiavellian Intelligence*. New York: Oxford University Press, 1988.

Dunbar, Robin and Louise Barrett. *Cousins*. London: DK Publishing, 2000.

Novak, Ronald. *Walker's Primates of the World*. Baltimore: Johns Hopkins University Press, 1999.

Peterson, Dale. *The Deluge and The Ark—A Journey into Primate Worlds*. Boston: Houghton Mifflin Co., 1989.

Preston-Mafham, Rod. *Primates of the World*. London: Blandford, 1999.

Sapolsky, Robert. *A Primate's Memoir*. New York: Scribner, 2002.

Shreeve, James. "Machiavellian Monkeys." *Discover*, June 1991.

Wilkinson, Richard H. *Reading Egyptian Art*. New York: Thames and Hudson, 1992.

Index

Page numbers in **boldface** are illustrations.

About the Author

Marc Zabludoff, former editor in chief of *Discover* magazine, has been involved in communicating science to the public for more than two decades. His other work for Marshall Cavendish includes *Spiders* and *Beetles* in the AnimalWays series and books on insects, reptiles, and the chiefly microscopic organisms known as protoctists in the Family Trees series. Zabludoff lives in New York City with his wife and daughter.